PACK LIGHTLY

BY
REBECCA
HARVIN

SLEEP NAKED

THE HANDBOOK TO MAKE TRAVEL EASIER, SAFER, AND SEXIER.

© Copyright 1997, by Rebecca Harvin, Henderson, NC
(919) 438-8849
Fax (919) 438-3762
E-Mail Address lharvin@mindspring.com

Cover & Book Design: Avery Designs, Clayton, NC

Cover & Text Illustrations: Russell Avery, Clayton, NC

Printed in the United States of America by Vaughan Printing, Nashville, TN.

DEDICATION

Though she might consider the title a bit risqué, I am dedicating this book to my mother, Bessie Evans Lane.

During all of our years of exciting travel, she made it often possible by being at home with my children. She not only had a career as an Executive Assistant to a corporate CEO, she was, and is, a wonderful mother, grandmother, and great-grandmother.

Knowing that my children, Rebecca, Ginnie, and Luke, were lovingly cared for while we traveled gave us great peace of mind and made our travels more enjoyable.

Thanks, Bessie.

I Love You,
Becky

INTRODUCTION

This book offers suggestions and advice for everyone who enjoys traveling.

Everything is covered: family vacations, business trips, honeymoons, and second honeymoons. From a short budget-controlled weekend to a lavish around-the-world tour and everything in between. It is all here!

Depending on what kind of trip you are making and how you like to travel, there are tips for everyone. If you are the kind of person who likes to change clothes ten times a day, well then take ten suitcases! If you prefer to travel light, get organized and travel with a backpack or one carry on.

The suggestions in this book can make travel easier, safer, and sexier for everyone. Use whatever applies or appeals to you and your personal whims. Make yourself happy, and have fun!

CONTENTS

I   Getting Ready   11
     Your Mind
     Your Body
     Your Wardrobe
     Packing
     Your House
     General

II   Helpful   33
     Resources
     Safety Tips
     Healthful
     Tips, Tidbits, and Trivia

III   Sensible and Sensuous   67

IV   The Healthy, Wealthy, and Wise
     —Mature Traveler Tips—   71

V   Are We There Yet?   77

VI   Traveling With Pets   89

VII   Eating While Traveling   95

VIII   Cruises and Special Interests   105

IX   Checklist   115
     Sitter
     Personal

GETTING READY

Your Mind

Your Body

Your Wardrobe

Packing

Your House

General Tips

GETTING READY

The best way to really enjoy traveling to the fullest is to get yourself ready. When I say yourself, I mean your body and your mind. Get mentally and physically fit and you are set to savor every minute of your trip without being pooped, frazzled, or confused.

MIND

Whether you are taking the children to Disneyland® or taking a romantic second honeymoon to Paris, prepare your mind months before you depart. Read and study about your destination. Learn, learn, learn everything you can about wherever you are going. Seek out what you want to see and should see. You never have time to see it all. For example, if you are surrounded with exceptional paintings, seek out the greatest masterpieces. Learn what to look for in great art. What made it famous—style, period, etc.? Familiarize yourself with the artist or artisan.

> Prepare your mind months before you depart. Learn, learn, learn everything you can about wherever you are going.

📠 Familiarize yourself with the history of the country, city, or resort you will be visiting

- 💼 Seek out special landmarks

- 💼 Plan what you will do and see. Obtain videos and cassettes on vacation locations.

- 💼 Ask your travel agent to get you information

- 💼 Search the "net"

However you prefer to do it, prepare your mind for a trip. You will enjoy and remember what you do and what you see one hundred percent more when you are even vaguely familiar with your surroundings.

BODY

Getting your body physically fit for a trip is as important as preparing your mind, maybe even more so. Without stamina, you tire quickly and miss too much.

Personally, I feel I am wasting my time and money if I miss anything; therefore, I try to save rest time for a boring day at home. An occasional siesta is permissible if needed!

Do those crunches. Lose a few Lbs. Let your body talk.

Consider the fact that on a vacation your roommate, whether your spouse, mistress, lover, girlfriend, boyfriend, or whomever, will be seeing more of your body! Enhance your trip by making your body as physically attractive as possible. Lose those pounds you have been talking about, and tighten that tummy. You will feel a lot better about yourself when you are dressing and undressing several times each day in front of your roommate!

If you are an old timer, your trip may likely turn into a second honeymoon! When your roommate happens not to be a significant other, you are more than likely to find one with your mind and body in top-notch shape. Just try it!

Whatever getting in shape means to you, do it—running, walking, tennis, biking, aerobics, etc.! Don't expect to be able to fully enjoy a busy vacation when your major activity is watching TV. As Olivia Newton-John says, "Get physical - let your body talk!"

Chapter III has more suggestions on getting your body ready, such as, buying new sexy underwear!

WARDROBE

Now that your mind and body are ready let's talk about organizing your wardrobe. A well planned wardrobe is especially important when you like to accessorize. Travelers who have multiple events to attend: seminars, sports events, all kinds of business and social events-casual and formal or just touring, should plan their dress with care.

> Organize your wardrobe in detail.

The only way to have an enjoyable trip, free from stressful indecisions of what to wear when, is to organize your wardrobe in detail. The following suggestions come from my personal experiences.

First and foremost, check seasonal temperatures, both night and day, of your destination so your clothing will be suitable for the climate. Being too hot or too cold can make any camper unhappy.

Begin preparing for your trip several days before you leave. Set aside a designated area or separate room in which to put everything that you intend to take. Whenever you go shopping for your trip—stockings, lingerie, etc., put them in this room or place instead of away in a drawer. Then, when you are ready to pack, everything is in one spot.

Most serious travelers have a specific itinerary. Use it when packing. Decide what you will wear to each event every day, and write it down. The itinerary is a good place to make your notes. As a matter of fact, the itinerary should be your checklist.

When you finish packing, be sure to take your list with you.

Remember, write your packing list down, and take it with you!

Your shoes will be your most important accessory when you will be doing lots of walking, dancing, or standing. Nothing can spoil a trip any quicker than hurting feet. Do not buy new shoes for a trip and pop them in your suitcase. Instead, wear them and make sure they are comfortable—a tried and true tip!

Always take walking shoes for trips with long excursions and tours. Look for shoes with the American Orthopedic Association Seal of Approval.

Include, and write down all other accessories for each outfit - belts, scarves, jewelry, etc. Deciding what you will wear with what two or three times a day can be very time consuming. Organize before you leave home and save your travel time for more fun things.

Planning and arranging your wardrobe will lighten your luggage load. While taking a "little too much" is permissible, hauling around tons of baggage is a pain.

One very important reason to know exactly what you will be wearing is the baggage storage available when you arrive. For example, on a cruise even the largest stateroom will accommodate only a few pieces of luggage. Baggage will also cramp a room! One of my most fun and memorable trips was on the Orient Express from Paris to Venice. The romantic, but tiny compartment required exact planning with only one small carry-on bag permitted. With formal dining on the itinerary, such a limitation presented a testy situation for someone who wanted to take it all! Planning permitted me

> Never even consider packing a suitcase until you have decided on everything you will take.

to coordinate the same accessories I wore on the train with my dress for later and I eliminated packing any extra shoes, belts, jewelry, etc.

When your baggage is limited, be creative with basic clothing. When more space is available, indulge yourself and enjoy changing clothes and dressing up. Being glamorous and prissy is part of the fun of traveling, especially without the children hanging around asking, "What's for dinner?"

Plan your wardrobe, and get organized before leaving. Do not spend time on a trip fussing over what to wear, and you will have more time for play and business. You will always look striking, you will not forget something important, and you will not be overloaded with things you do not want or need.

Now that you know what you are taking, let's get you packing.

PACKING

Never even consider packing a suitcase until you have decided on everything you will take.

Once you have your wardrobe all settled, here are some helpful packing tips:

- Before you pack, remove all previous airport tags from suitcase handles and from outside of suitcases

- Pack socks and stockings in shoes

- Pack heavy items on bottom

- Roll soft clothes such as lingerie and sweaters

- Close all buttons, zippers, and straps

- Pack dresses, skirts, and slacks lengthwise or roll them

- Stuff empty spaces with accessories, socks, underwear, etc.

- Pack as flatly as possible. The less you fold, the more you will get into a suitcase and the fewer wrinkles you will have.

- 🧳 Put a layer of tissue paper between outfits (this takes a lot of tissue paper, but keeps more wrinkles out)

- 🧳 Use a hanging bag if you prefer

Pack one of your outfits in your companion's suitcase and one of theirs in yours. If one bag is lost or delayed, you will have at least one change of clothes. When traveling alone, always pack an extra outfit in your carry-on bag.

If possible, pack in matching luggage. You will look neater, you will not have to identify but one kind of luggage and you can borrow your spouse's luggage. Also distinctive ribbons or tassels on the handles help identify your bag.

Pack small items such as toiletries, underwear, socks, ties, belts, make-up, etc., in separate see through bags. I like to use zip-lock bags or a travel valet. Never pack small items loose!

Always pack liquids that might leak in zip-lock bags.

Pack travelers checks, airline tickets, passports, visas, documents, money and any valuables in a safe, secure place in your carry-on bags, briefcase, or money belt.

Always pack a pair of jeans and tennis shoes!

Leave valuable jewelry at home. Carry faux jewelry when traveling. If you take expensive jewelry, keep it with you while traveling.

Pack film in a lead bag. This will protect it from dust, water, and airport x-rays.

Have an attractive carry-on bag. This makes you a much neater-looking traveler.

Always pack an extra duffel bag or expandable bag for all the goodies you bring home.

Use your checklist when packing. Whenever you forget something, add it to your list. Make your own checklist on the convenient spaces added in the back of this book. Keep this list handy on your closet door or mirror.

Be sure to pack your toothpaste, shampoos, etc. These little sundries are very costly at resorts and they never have your favorite brand anyway. Remember, these are the items to put in zip-lock bags.

Take travel-size toiletries and make-up. They take up much less room.

Always pack ID on the inside of your luggage.

Ski bags, golf bags, and tennis bags are wonderful places to pack dirty clothes when returning home!

Pick and pack lightweight and wrinkle resistant clothing. Layer these to adjust to night and day temperatures.

Try not to pack a zillion pair of shoes. Instead, try the following:

For Women Only

- 1 pair flat heel shoes or sandals that go with everything
- 1 pair heels that go with everything
- 1 pair evening shoes - usually gold or bronze
- 1 pair of shoes for a special outfit
- 1 pair of walking shoes

Total = 5 pair of shoes
(Pack 4; wear either your walking shoes or the pair that goes with everything.)

Never pack more carry-on luggage than you can handle with ease, not more than 2 items, one for each hand. Too many carry-ons make you look very unorganized and messy, and you are guaranteed to drop one piece at least once!

CHECKLIST FOR YOUR CARRY-ON BAG

Tickets _____

Medications _____

Basic Make-up _____

Tooth & Hair Brush _____

Any Valuable Jewelry _____

Glasses and Contacts _____

Toothpaste _____

Passports, Visa, ID _____

Credit Cards _____

One Change of Clothes _____

Camera, if Room _____

Any Essentials You Need _____

Anything You Would

Hate to Lose or

Could not Replace _____

Guard Your Carry-on Bag Tenaciously!!

YOUR HOUSE

- Suspend newspapers & mail temporarily

- Leave a house key with a neighbor

- Arrange for pet care

- Arrange for yard maintenance

- Set house alarm system

- Make sure answering machines and faxes are on

> Make sure your children are well taken care of.

- Leave babysitters all important information-see page 115 for my convenient forms

- Secure all windows and doors

- Clean your house before you leave or have someone clean it after you leave. Make sure to leave fresh linens and towels.

- Have your mail and bills up to date

- Have someone water your plants

- Clean out refrigerator

- Empty all trash

- Leave your itinerary with someone responsible

- Set timers on lights in several rooms

- Unplug small appliances

- Turn down thermostats

- If you are traveling for an extended time, have someone check your house regularly

GENERAL TIPS

When you are not traveling with your children, make arrangements for them to be well cared for. This preparation will be the most important decision you make for a relaxing trip.

Selecting a destination that accommodates your wants is a good first step to planning the successful vacation. Take time to research the perfect location for your trip. The internet is a wonderful resource to help you plan your trip; however, I still prefer to consult with my travel agent.

Anti-Jet-Lag Diet
Argonne National Laboratory
Office of Public Affairs
Box 201
9700 S. Cass Avenue
Argonne, IL 60439

When selecting a hotel, make sure it is not going through renovation or some other kind of construction work.

Get into extra good shape physically for strenuous vacations, such as skiing, hiking, biking, riding, etc.

When taking a physically strenuous trip, pack your old tired underwear. After wearing, throw it away!

Get vaccinations early. Vaccinations often cause reactions and fever.

Read "1001 Ways to be Romantic," and "365 Ways to Improve your Sex Life" before you leave!

Purchase traveler's checks.

Obtain plenty of small bills for tips, etc.

Always carry your business card.

Allow 4-6 weeks for renewed or new passports. Don't wait until the last minute to get your passport.

If you get in a passport or visa crunch and need one quickly, contact:
Travisa 1 (800) 222-2589

One of my favorite travel tips: If you like to send post cards and want to save a lot of time, print (or have your secretary print) all your family and friends' names and addresses on computer labels before you leave. When you are ready to send a post card, no getting out the address book and looking up everyone's address. Just peel, stick, and mail! Don't forget to pack stamps, too! This makes a wonderful bon voyage gift.

AIRLINE TIPS

Call your airline the day of departure, before leaving, to confirm flight times. You will avoid unnecessary delays at the airport. Be sure to do this in the event of bad weather.

Always re-confirm 24 hours in advance:

- ✈ Airline reservations
- ✈ Airline seating
- ✈ Hotel reservations
- ✈ Car rentals
- ✈ Transportation arrangements

When traveling during a busy season, make your reservations early. Flights for holidays sometimes sell out months ahead of time. Don't miss Thanksgiving dinner with the family!

Book reservations early for the best deals.

Redeem frequent flyer miles early.

If you need a wheelchair, make the request when you make your reservations.

The basic rule for getting the best airfare is to purchase your ticket 14 days in advance and stay over a Saturday night.

When checking your baggage have your ID handy.

If you are taking a long flight with a significant time change, you may want to follow an anti-jet lag program. Several books are available that will explain what you must do. This program usually takes about three days, so allow yourself enough time. For a copy of the anti-jet lag diet, write:

Anti-Jet Lag Diet
Argonne National Laboratory
Office of Public Affairs
Box 201
9700 S. Cass Avenue
Argonne, IL 60439

Remember that you can order, in advance, special airline meals—no fat, sugar-free, vegetarian, or special children's meals. Order your preference when you make your reservations.

Read "1001 Ways to be Romantic," and "365 Ways to Improve your Sex Life" before you leave!

ANYTHING I FORGOT?

_____

_____

_____

_____

_____

_____

_____

_____

_____

_____

_____

_____

_____

_____

HELPFUL

The most helpful tip I can give computer literates is to use the internet. The internet has opened up the world to us. If you are a computer user, hit the information highway and plan your travels. You can obtain information on anything and anywhere on the World Wide Web.

If you don't want to communicate with a screen, do it my way and consult with your favorite travel agent. They will conveniently do all the work for you with a human touch. I prefer the human touch in more ways than one!

RESOURCES

Helpful telephone numbers and addresses:

☎ U.S. Department of State 202-647-5225 (lists travel conditions and warnings, consular information)

☎ Washington Passport Agency 202-647-0518 or:
Washington Passport Agency
1425 K Street NW
Washington, DC 20522-1705

For information on: vaccination requirements, current disease outbreaks worldwide and AIDS in foreign travel, and other pertinent disease information contact:

☎ Centers for Disease Control 404-332-4559

To report lost or stolen credit cards call:

☎ Mastercard
1-800-622-7747 or
1-303-278-8000 cfa*

☎ Diner's Club
1-800 234-6377 or
1-303-790-2433 cfa*

☎ American Express
1-800-528-4800 or
1-910-333-3211 cfa*

☎ Visa   1-800-336-8472 or
                          1-410-581-7931 cfa*

☎ Discover   1-800-347-2683
(only accepted in U.S.)
*cfa - collect from abroad

If you lose your credit card and do not know the toll-free number to report your card stolen, call toll-free directory information: 1-800-555-1212.

Join AARP when eligible. They give discounts on car rentals, hotels, resorts, restaurants, and numerous other things.

☎ AARP membership and | Join AARP
general inquires 1-800-424- | when eligible.
3410

☎ AARP tour information 1-800-927-0111

☎ AARP cruise information 1-800-745-4567
(This is a great way for single seniors to travel. You may not be single for long!)

Join the AAA motor club if you drive frequently. They offer terrific benefits for the motorist, such as emergency road services, travel agency services, and discounts on numerous items; including, traveler's checks, cruises, hotels, tours, rental cars, security systems and much more.

AAA Motor Club 1-800-477-4222

Passport applications are available at US passport agencies and many post offices. Or write:

Washington Passport Agency
1425 K Street NW
Washington, DC 20522-1705
202-647-0518

Some travel agencies specialize in vacations for people with disabilities. Call:

Travel Information Service of Moss Rehab
Hospital 215-456-9600

Honeymoon Magazine—a guide to choosing a destination. Call 1-800-513-7112.

Traveling for Two: The Pregnant Traveler I urge you to get a copy of this report if you or anyone you know is expecting and traveling. It's $5 from:

Traveling Healthy
108-48 70th Rd
Forest Hills, NY 11375
718-268-7290

Watch the PBS series, National Explorer Channel, a great way to learn about unusual places, people, animals, etc.

Each state has a division of tourism. Locate the number in your state, and use it concerning questions about a particular state.

The Travel Channel, available on many cable networks,

In a crunch for a quick passport or visa, call Travisa 1 (800) 222-2589.

runs programs devoted to travel throughout the day and night.

The Weather Channel runs traveler's weather updates.

Check the travel section of your newspaper for travel shows on television. You will see many great travel programs. The Learning Channel and CNN Travelguide are two I recommend.

Regularly read the Sunday travel section of your newspaper. You will see:

Special air fares
Weather—National and International
Exchange rates
Articles about places you never dreamed of
visiting
Special hotel rates
Budget tips
Much, much more

Read travel magazines—<u>Travel and Leisure</u>, <u>Conde Naste</u>, etc.

When traveling, always keep your mind open to new thoughts and new adventures.

Especially good books (other than mine) for travelers:
<u>Fordois</u>
<u>Frommeis</u>

One book I recommend for the traveler who has already been everywhere and already has everything is <u>Wild Planet! 1,001 Extraordinary Events for the Inspired Traveler</u> by Tom Clynes.

Check special events that will be going on wherever you are going. The Chamber of Commerce is a good resource.

If you need a doctor, most yellow pages have a local emergency number.

Make an effort to speak basic phrases in the language of any country. Toss perfection aside, smile, use facial expressions and body language, and have a sense of humor. You will get

Be sure you know what you should and should not eat and drink in a foreign country.

your answer and you will so enjoy interaction with another culture.

Here are basic phrases in eight different languages that are always helpful:

English	Spanish
Good day	Buenos dias
How are you?	Como esta usted?
Yes	Si
No	No
Please	Por favor
Thank you	Gracias
Excuse me	Perdoneme
What time is it?	Que hora es?
Where is the hotel?	Donde esta el hotel?
Where is the train station?	Donde esta la estacion de ferrocarril?
Where is the bank?	Donde esta el banco?
Where is the toilet?	Donde estan los servicios?
I would like something to eat.	Quisiera algo de corner.
How much does it cost?	Cuanto cuesta?
Do you have a room?	Tiene usted habitaciones libres?
I don't speak Spanish.	No hablo espanol.

English	French
Good day	Bonjour
How are you?	Comment allezvous?
Yes	Oui
No	Non
Please	S'il vous plait
Thank you	Merci
Excuse me	Excusiz-moi/Pardon
What time is it?	Quelle heure estil?
Where is the hotel?	Ou est l'hotel?
Where is the train station?	Ou est la gare?
Where is the bank?	Ou est la banque?
Where is the toilet?	Ou sont les toilettes?
I would like something to eat.	Je voudrais quelque chose a manager.
How much does it cost?	Combien coute-t-il?
Do you have a room?	Avez-vous des chambres disponibles?
I don't speak French.	Je ne parle pas francais.

English	German
Good day	Guten Tag
How are you?	Wie geht es Ihnen?
Yes	Ja
No	Nein
Please	Bitte
Thank you	Danke
Excuse me	Enfschuldigen Sie bitte
What time is it?	Wieviel Uhr ist es?
Where is the hotel?	Wo ist das Hotel, bitte?
Where is the train station?	Wo ist der Bahnhof, bitte?
Where is the bank?	Wo ist die Bank, bitte?
Where is the toilet?	Wo is die Toilette, bitte?
I would like something to eat.	Ich moechte essen.
How much does it cost?	Wieviel kostet das?
Do you have a room?	Haben Sie ein Zimmer?
I don't speak German.	Ich spreche kein Deutsch.

English	Italian
Good day	Buon giorno
How are you?	Come sta?
Yes	Si
No	No
Please	Per favore
Thank you	Grazie
Excuse me	Mi scusi
What time is it?	Che ore sono?
Where is the hotel?	Dov'e l'albergo?
Where is the train station?	Dov'e la stazione?
Where is the bank?	Dov'e la banca?
Where is the toilet?	Dov'e il gabinetto?
I would like something to eat.	Vorrei mangiare qualcosa.
How much does it cost?	Quanto costa?
Do you have a room?	Avete camere libere?
I don't speak Italian.	Non parlo italiano.

English	Norwegian
Good day	God dag
How are you?	Hvordan star det til?
Yes	Ja
No	Nei
Please	Vennligst
Thank you	Mange takk
Excuse me	Unnskyld meg
What time is it?	Hvor mange er klokken?
Where is the hotel?	Hvor er hotellet?
Where is the train station?	Hvor ligger jernbanestasjonen?
Where is the bank?	Hvor ligger banken?
Where is the toilet?	Hvor er det et toalett?
I would like something to eat.	Jeg vil gjerne ha noe og spise.
How much does it cost?	Hvor mye koster det?
Do you have a room?	Har Det et vaereise?
I don't speak Norwegian.	Jeg snakker ikke Norsk.

English	Russian
Good day	Dobraye utra
How are you?	Kak vashi dila?
Yes	Da
No	Nyet
Please	Pazhalusta
Thank you	Spasiba
Excuse me	Prastitye pazhalusta
What time is it?	Katoryi chas?
Where is the hotel?	Gde gastinitsy?
Where is the train station?	Gde vagzala?
Where is the bank?	Gde bank?
Where is the toilet?	Skazhitye pazhalusta gdye tualyet?
I would like something to eat.	Ya by khatyel syest.
How much does it cost?	S kolka eta stoit?
Do you have a room?	Ya by khatyel nomir?
I don't speak Russian.	Ya ni gavaryu pa-ruski.

English	Japanese
English	**Japanese**
Good day	Konnichiwa
How are you?	Ogenki desu ka?
Yes	Hai
No	Iie
Please	Doozo
Thank you	Arigatoo gozaimasu
Excuse me	Sumimasen
What time is it?	Ima nan-ji desu ka?
Where is the hotel?	Hoteru wa doko desu ka?
Where is the train station?	Tetsudo no eki wa doko desu ka?
Where is the bank?	Ginko wa koko desu ka?
Where is the toilet?	Senmenjo wa doko desu ka?
I would like something to eat.	Nanika tabetei no desu ga.
How much does it cost?	Ikura desu ka?
Do you have a room?	Aita heya wa arimasu ka?
I don't speak Japanese.	Nihongo wa hanasemasen.

English	Chinese
Good day	Ni hao
How are you?	Ni hao ma?
Yes	Shi
No	Bu shi
Please	Qing
Thank you	Xiexie
Excuse me	Duibuqi
What time is it?	Xianzai ji dian?
Where is the hotel?	Luguan zai nali?
Where is the train station?	Huoche zhan zai nali?
Where is the bank?	Yinhang zai nali?
Where is the toilet?	Cesuo zai nali?
I would like something to eat.	Wo xiang chi fan.
How much does it cost?	Duoshao qian?
Do you have a room?	Ni zher you kong fangijian ma?
I don't speak Chinese.	Wo bu hui shuo hanyu.

If you prefer to pursue a language in greater depth, basic language tapes and books for travelers are widely available. Or use the internet Foreign Languages for Travelers at http://www.travlang.com/languages.

Helpful Internet Sites

▣ NBC News Intellicast World Weather: http://www.Intellicast.Com/weather

YAHOO : http://www.yahoo.com/Recreation/Travel

For instant driving directions to any town in the United States and Canada, go to Trip Quest. Type in your starting point and destination. This internet site will then calculate the distance of your trip and give you detailed written directions.

▣ Map Quest! Interactive Atlas: http: // www.Mapquest.Com/

This internet service will give you customized maps. Type in the place you wish to visit, what you are interested in—shops, restaurants, museums, hotels, etc.,and Map Quest! Interactive Atlas will draw a map.

These spaces are for you to keep your favorite internet sites that will inevitably occur.

Note: Internet addresses change frequently. A check of search engines will provide a multitude of travel related locations.

_____

_____

_____

_____

_____

_____

_____

_____

_____

_____

_____

_____

SAFETY TIPS

Using your business address on luggage tags instead of your home address helps prevent potential burglary. You will not be advertising your home is "home alone."

The Association of Flight Attendants teaches that clothing can make a differ-

"Remember. In an underdeveloped country, don't drink the water; in a developed country, don't breathe the air."
Changing Times Magazine

ence between life and death in the event of an emergency. Travel in comfortable, attractive, and safe clothing. Avoid wearing clothing made of flammable synthetic materials such as polyester. Cotton clothing is a better choice. Pantyhose would melt on your body in the event of fire.

High heels and sandals can slow down an emergency escape. Closed shoes are a better choice.

Casual dress is not necessarily safer than being dressed up. It's the materials in the clothing that make the difference.

Keep small bills for tips and cabs in a special place, so you do not have to expose large bills and everything else in your wallet or briefcase.

If you are traveling alone, consider group tours for more safety, security, and companionship. This may even lead to an exciting relationship. Who knows?

Lock all windows and doors to outside and to connecting rooms.

Place all valuables in a safe deposit box.

Do not draw attention to yourself by wearing expensive jewelry and displaying large amounts of cash.

Do not leave guest room keys in public places such as restaurants, swimming pools, etc. They may be stolen.

In foreign countries and cities, ask the concierge of your hotel to write the name and address of your hotel in the local language. Carry this with you at all times. I have gotten into frantic trouble several times because I could not make a taxi driver understand my Southern English language!

Wear rubber sole shoes on ship decks and any slippery surfaces.

Be sure to use sunscreen and be aware of your amount of sun exposure.

FIRE SAFETY

When you first arrive, locate fire exits and stairways wherever you are staying.

Try to keep a flashlight handy.

Make a note of the local fire and police department numbers. Find out how to dial these numbers.

Never use an elevator when there is a fire.

In the event of fire, touch the doorknob before opening the door. If it is not hot, open the door slowly and go to the nearest exit.

If your door is hot, DO NOT OPEN IT. Remain in your room. Block cracks under the doors. Run water in the tubs and sinks. Soak towels and put them over your face.

Stay near the floor.

If you are on a ship, you will have to participate in a lifeboat drill. Pay close attention! Review your instructions, which will be in your stateroom.

HEALTHFUL

Eat sensibly.

Pig out occasionally.

Wear "medical alert" devices if needed.

Never put essential medicines in checked baggage. Keep them with you.

Always bring a sufficient supply of prescription medicines.

Request non-smoking accommodations, when desired.

Stay at a hotel with a fitness facility and/or pool, or find the nearest YMCA, YWCA, or fitness center. Y's usually have reciprocal agreements.

Use the stairs instead of the elevator.

Go walking, jogging, biking.

Pack a jump rope.

Bring your favorite fitness tape.

Walk in airports when you have layovers.

Attend early morning exercise groups.

When you are traveling on a business trip, use the break as an exercise break instead of coffee and donuts.

When you cannot exercise while traveling, forget about it and enjoy your vacation. Get back into your routine as soon as you return from your trip.

Seek out doctors' references and locations before you leave.

Remember, Medicare does not provide medical insurance outside the U.S.

Check your medical insurance policies before you leave. You may need to purchase additional insurance before traveling abroad.

When planning a cruise, get motion sickness medication if needed.

To avoid common stomach upsets when traveling in foreign countries:

- Eat only fruits and vegetables that you can peel, and peel them before eating

- Do not drink tap water

- Always order bottled water in restaurants and open it yourself

- Do not brush your teeth with tap water

- Keep your mouth closed in the shower

- Do not order mixed drinks with water

If you are an international traveler, this internet address would be most helpful and healthful:

Shoreland's
Travel Health Online - The home of travel health and safety on the World Wide Web.
http://www.tripprep.com/index.html
This site will review topics such as:
- General Travel Health Concerns
- Preventive Medications & Vaccines
- Summaries of Travel Illnesses

TIPS, TIDBITS, AND TRIVIA

Purchase luggage with wheels. This makes it wonderfully easy to carry your own luggage!

If your traveler's checks do not have a receipt with a list of all the checks in each packet, make a list of them yourself before you leave home. Write down the number printed in the top right-hand corner of the check and its denomination. Keep this list separate from the traveler's checks.

Bring a pocket calculator.

Before you leave home, buy a small amount of currency of the country you are visiting.

To get the best exchange rate, compare bank rates, hotel rates, and airport rates.

Ask for a refrigerator in your room if needed.

Order an iron and iron-ing board and press all wrin-kled garments right away. Be done with it and get that unsightly ironing board out of your room.

Always take advantage of cultural and ethnic opportunities.

Never leave your car keys in checked baggage.

Always bring surprises to the children, mother, mother-in-law, housekeepers, sitters, secretary, etc. Take an extra bag to hold all these goodies.

Most hotels and resorts have faxes and computers. Use them.

Remember, these three words are recognized interna-tionally!

Corn Flakes

■ Coca Cola

■ Preparation H

Always travel in something comfortable and attractive.

Familiarize yourself with the money exchange in a foreign country. Use your pocket computer to help you convert.

When shopping, remember to ship your purchases home. You save lugging them around and you may not have to pay state taxes. More importantly, your spouse will never know you went shopping...until the bill arrives!

Don't be a frumpy-looking traveler. Airlines, restaurants, shops, theaters, museums, etc., appreciate a neat traveler.

Carry an extra pair of contact lenses or glasses.

Carry your eyeglasses' prescription.

In foreign countries, it is wise to have your own feminine supplies.

Never run out of film.

Always pack something for a headache.

Always carry identification.

If you have a long ride or flight, being a frugivorous traveler is beneficial.

Always carry cash and traveler's checks.

Always carry small bills for tips.

Have trip insurance.

Have trip cancellation insurance.

When traveling via car:

- Take projects that you never seem to get around to, such as organizing picture albums and going through all those catalogs and magazines that have accumulated

- Always take a cooler in the car with water, sodas, etc. This will save time.

- Reserve audio books at the public library to take with you

- In cold weather, always have a candle, matches, flashlight, and blanket

- Have a cellular phone

- Rest every three hours

Avoid mini-bar snacks. They are costly and usually full of fat.

Mini-bar = Maxi cost

You can eliminate enormous long-distance charges by calling collect or using a calling card. When abroad, dial AT&T USA Direct Service, MCI or Sprint, depending on which carrier you use.

Charging a long-distance call to your room is usually unwise. Hotels generally use telephone departments as profit centers and often charge 5-10 times the cost of a long-distance call.

Bereavement fares are normally not as inexpensive as supersaver or advance purchase coach fares, but they are much less expensive than the normal business traveler fares. Ask for them when needed.

Keep a travel journal or diary. Fond memories are fun to recall.

Try to find local tour guides. They are usually more colorful and add a special charm to sometimes boring tours.

Always ask for help whenever you feel you need it. You will usually find strangers very friendly and helpful.

Visit your National Parks.

Stay in a neat bed and breakfast when appropriate.

Everyone knows how to spend, but do you know what to buy?

Always take advantage of cultural and ethnic opportunities.

Strive to see something you've never seen before, learn something new, and eat something you've never eaten before.

Whenever you have an opportunity, go to the museums.

The worst days in the year to fly are Tuesday and Wednesday before Thanksgiving and the following Sunday and Monday.

When touring a new city, go to the highest point on the first day. This will give you a good perspective of the surrounding area. For example, if in Paris for the first time, visit the Eiffel Tower first; New York City, World Trade Towers.

Know what to buy. Find out what is the best buy in a particular country or city. Bring your own shopping bag. Some countries do not give you a bag for your merchandise.

If you are traveling on your own with a group of friends, instead of trying to reach an agreement among 6-8 people on what you will do each day, where you will eat, etc., let each couple plan a day. This eliminates confusion and everyone can enjoy several days without any responsibility. You will enjoy being surprised with the itinerary.

> Resorts may have spas, but spas do not frequently contain resorts.

Make reservations early for special events you want to see.

On long airplane trips, get comfortable. Ask for pillows, blankets, magazines, music, etc. Drink lots of water, eat lightly, stretch occasionally, and enjoy getting there. Just before arrival, brush your teeth and hair, wash your face and hands, and redo make-up.

A resort offers enough activities on its own properties so guests do not have to go elsewhere.

> Always ask for your senior discount.

A spa is like a resort with a focus on health and fitness. Resorts may have spas, but spas do not frequently contain resorts.

If your flight is delayed for a lengthy time, take a free hotel shuttle to the nearest and best hotel or resort. Enjoy touring the resort, and enjoy a nice meal. You can even get "day rooms" at reasonable rates. With a day room, you can relax in the pool or spa. When you return to the terminal, everyone will wonder how you manage to look restful and unstressed.

Be creative. Utilize your time when a flight is postponed, late, or delayed:

- ✈ Read a good book

- ✈ Take a long walk

- ✈ Write your post cards

- ✈ Get a shoe shine

- ✈ Make a new friend

- ✈ Have your pictures developed at an airport one-hour express photo and enjoy them!

- ✈ Surf the net

- ✈ Catch up on some work with your laptop

When I have just attended a seminar, I love to review all my notes. I get them organized and write letters. When I get home, I can relax for a while.

Now that you are loaded with tips, tidbits, and trivia let me get to the sensible and sensuous.

> Whenever you are a house guest, always take a gift. This book would be perfect!

SENSIBLE AND SENSUOUS

Although this section is my shortest, I consider it the most important for a sexcessful trip with a significant other.

Remember, a little means a lot—a little perfume, a little wine, a little underwear.

Try these little tips. I think you will make your vacation a renewal of life, love, and living:

Leave the children at home.

Scatter perfume samples throughout your suitcase.

Don't get a new hairdo right before a trip. Stick with one you know you like and that you can handle.

Make sure your hair is cut and colored before you leave on a trip. Cuts and color are too chancy with someone new. A bad hair week can ruin a vacation!

Have your nails done, fingers and toes.

When staying at resort hotels, spas, etc., make appointments in advance for massages, facials, hair, nails, whatever. If you wait until you arrive and want an appointment, these salons will be booked.

Pamper yourself on vacation.

Go dancing, wining and dining.

Remember, a little means a lot—a little perfume, a little wine, a little underwear.

Dress up in your sexiest clothes.

Order the champagne but —-don't sip it in the Jacuzzi or hot tub too long!

Pack your see through robe.

Always buy new lingerie.

Take a new perfume.

Make sure you lose those few pounds and do those crunches before you leave.

Sleep late.

Take a nap.

Read a sexy novel.

Shave your legs—twice a day.

Wear sunscreen.

Plan a weekend vacation during a full moon to some romantic spot.

Go to the opera for an evening.

Make love a lot.

Go to the museums together.

Be sure that you drink fine wine and Scotch.

Order breakfast in bed.

Don't call home every day.

Don't call the office every day.

When you arrive at your destination, put away your briefcase and computer for good.

Get to know your spouse or traveling partner. Share feelings while you have some time together.

Have a second honeymoon.

Enjoy yourself and your partner.

Sleep naked. Saves time and space!

THE HEALTHY, WEALTHY, AND WISE

—MATURE TRAVELER TIPS—

—MATURE TRAVELER TIPS—

This section is devoted to the mature traveler, the healthy, wealthy, and wise group.

Before retirement, your travel experiences were often limited to business trips or family vacations. Now it is time for you to enjoy travel more than ever!

You are not limited because of age to anything or any kind of travel. Do whatever you can handle. Go wherever you desire.

> Travels with grandchildren develop close relationships that will make a difference in your lives.

Enjoy this time of your life by exploring new opportunities and challenges and expanding your horizons.

The dog died and the children are grown! You worked for it. You deserve it. So get going!

Following is a list of resources:

- Elderhostel—group trips designed for elders in the US and foreign countries. The organization balances adventure travel, educational travel, and budget prices. Elderhostels have even been likened to Outward Bound programs and offer white water rafting.

For a complete description of Elerhostel programs:
Elderhostel
75 Federal St.
Boston, Mass 02110 or call
617-426-8056

You may specify domestic or international.

▋▋ Elder Treks-a new brochure describing 20 tours in
14 countries designed for the 50+ age group. Each
tour is limited to 15 travelers, is fully escorted, and
ranges from 10-29 days. For exciting cruises and
trips, call
800-741-7956
416-588-5000

▋▋ Walking the World focuses on the outdoor life for
those 50+—very adventurous! Example: walks
through a rain forest, white water rafting, etc. For
information, call 800-340-9255.

▋▋ Outdoor Vacations for Women over 40—a tour
company for solo women or groups of women. For
a free brochure, call 508-448-3331.

An excellent book that suggests new ways to see the
world: <u>Travel and Learn, Where to Go For Everything
You'd Love to Know</u> (Blue Penguin Publications, 1994).

Motor coach trips are very popular because the mature traveler has more time. For a free copy of <u>20 Consumer Protection Tips for Chartering a Motor Coach</u>, write:

National Motor Coach Network
Patriot Square 10527C
Braddock Road
Fairfax, VA 22032

Cruises have always been popular vacations for young and wise travelers. My last section is devoted to cruises. If you really want to perk up a relationship, you may want to look into a cruise with Bare Necessities or Au Natural! Section VIII will give you more details.

One of the greatest pleasures I have gained from being a wiser traveler is traveling with my grandchildren. Traveling with grandchildren has become a growing industry. Traveling with a grandchild will be a very special experience. Travels with grandchildren develop close relationships that will make a wonderful difference in your lives. Try one of these for a trip with your grandchild:

- Grandtravel-offers grand trips and the tours are divided according to the ages of children, 7-11 and 12-17. Call 800-247-7651 (more expensive).

- Elderhostel's Grandchild Programs offer everything from outdoor challenging survival programs to quieter liberal arts tours.

Call 617-426-7788 or 617-426-8056 or Fax 617-426-8351 (budget prices)

For Elderhostel on the net, go to

http://www.deepriver.com/adven/htm/1237.htm, or http://www.elderhostel.org/

A Disney Theme Park is a popular place to take grandchildren. See Section Five for Disney tips.

Don't kid yourself either, Walt Disney World® is a wonder world for adults!

"ARE WE THERE YET?"

Traveling with children is lots of fun and important for a family; however, taking the children is a whole different ball game from traveling with a significant other! You will probably want to skip my sensuous section and leave the see through robes at home!

Be sure to prepare your children for their trips, too. I like to have an itinerary for all my trips, but when traveling with children, planning is especially important.

A good itinerary helps you visualize your vacation before you leave home. With children, this visualization is particularly important, and you will enjoy a

> Educate your children about dealing with strangers. You can never protect your children too much in public places.

well planned and hassle-free vacation.

Theme parks and cities are popular family vacation destinations, because they offer action and entertainment for both children and grown ups.

Although the most popular theme parks in the United States are Disney World® or some Disney theme park, these tips can apply to any park or public place you take your children.

THEME PARK TIPS

- Don't take children too young

- Make sure children have visible ID with them

- Pick up a map at the park's entrance that locates all the bathrooms and diaper changing and bottle-warming stations

- Choose what you see wisely. Make sure your children will enjoy and not be frightened.

- ☃ Pack sunscreen, lip balm, and wear sun hats

- ☃ Plan ahead. Know which rides and shows your family will enjoy.

- ☃ Make a lunch reservation as soon as you arrive at the park. Plan your morning so that you end up at this restaurant at lunch time—no waiting in line, no unhappy children, or parents.

> Enjoy traveling with your children and take lots of pictures. Travel creates special bonds between siblings and with parents. You will forever cherish these times together.

- ☃ Plan to ride the most popular attractions when the park opens or after 6 p.m., when the motor coach groups usually depart

- ☃ Start at the back of the park when it opens—unless you think too many others have read the same book and know this tip! In that case, proceed to the middle of the park and work your way out in a spiral.

- ☃ If the children become hot or tired, find a show that everyone will enjoy in an air-conditioned theater

- ☃ Wear a fanny pack. These are much easier to take on rides and also much harder to misplace.

- Take frequent breaks with water, lemonade, ice cream, etc.

- Educate your children about dealing with strangers. You can never protect your children too much in public places.

DISNEY TIPS

- Dress small children in clothes with their name on it in large print. They will be thrilled when Mickey Mouse® and everyone else knows them by name!

- Dress in comfortable cotton clothing that dries quickly after a water ride or a rain shower

- Visit on a weekday when least crowded

- Least crowded time to go—November to mid-December

- Most crowded time—summer

- September and October weekends are great, too. You can see as much in one-and-a-half days during this time as you would four crowded summer days.

- If you go during the spring or summer when it is crowded, arrive early. Leave at noon, and relax at your hotel pool in the hot afternoon. Return about dark when the crowds have left.

Guide Books that will help you plan your trip to a Disney World Resort®:

- 🧳 Fodor's Walt Disney World® For Adults by Rita Aero-$14

- 🧳 Bernbaum's the Official Guide to Walt Disney World® by Stephen Bernbaum (Hyperion 12.95)

- 🧳 The Unofficial Guide to Walt Disney World® by Bob Sehlinger (MacMillan Travel $14)

- 🧳 Econoguide to Walt Disney World®, Epcot® and Universal Studios® by Corey Sandler (Long Meadow Press 8.95)

For more Disney information, write:

Disney World®
PO Box 10040
Lake Buena Vista, FL 32830
Or call 407-824-4321.

Visit Disney reports on the World Wide Web at http://206.232.42.10/vacations.htm, or http://www.disney.com/disney home page

If you are visiting Walt Disney World®, call 800-831-1844 for the Central Florida Discount Travel Guide.

AIRLINES AND CHILDREN

Give children their own small luggage with wheels. Children can manage these easily and they think they have a new pet.

Most airlines will reserve the seat next to you if you are traveling with an infant. That seat will only be used if the flight is full.

If you are planning to send your child on a flight alone:

✈ ♟ Try to get a direct flight

✈ ♟ Be aware that airlines usually charge $20 to $30 additional if your child is traveling alone

✈ ♟ Make sure your child's seat is located where they can easily be seen by an attendant

✈ ♟ Children 5-7 can fly unaccompanied on direct non-stop flights only

✈ ♟ See that your child has assistance changing planes if needed

✈ ♟ Never book a late evening flight

✈ ♟ Make sure your child has spending money

✈ 👶 Make sure your child has ID, destination, flight numbers, schedule; and parents or guardian name, address, and phone number

✈ 👶 Let the airline crew know if this is the child's first flight

✈ 👶 Let children know who will pick them up

✈ 👶 Person picking up child must have proper ID

Yummy news for children—most airlines offer peanut butter and jelly sandwiches. United Airlines offers McDonald's Friendly Skies Meals for children. USAir offers chicken legs and tater tots, and Delta serves pizza! Order your child's favorite.

CHILDREN AND MUSEUM

My five grandchildren have taught me that museums are special places. Museums are no longer no-touch, no-talk, dull displays in musty old buildings as they once were.

Museums and Science Technology Centers are now lively, bright, and entertaining, as well as educational places for children and parents.

Museums encourage hands-on, feet-on, minds-on, play, talk, laughter, etc. Discovery rooms are very popular where children can touch and discover on their own.

There are over 80 major children's museums in the United States. I definitely would ask where they are located, and put them high on my list when taking a family trip. You can always go to a museum rain or shine.

The Association of Youth Museums can provide information on the location of children's museums.

Phone 202-466-4144.

E-mail - aymdc@aol.com

ON THE ROAD—WITH CHILDREN

Driving with your family can be a nightmare. With a little extra planning and organization, it can be a memorable and pleasant trip. We all prefer the later and pursuing some of my suggestions can work wonders.

- 🚗 Many travel agents and tour operators combine an airline ticket and rental car. This is called Fly/Drive option. Check this out. I think it would be an ideal way to take a family vacation. The Fly/Drive vacation lets you fly over the long, boring parts and drive the interesting and fun parts. Just the thing for children.

- 🚗 When convenient, take bikes, boats, skis, any favorite toys, etc.

- 🚗 Let children take a friend

🚗 When traveling via car, use this time for family conversations and discussions. This is a great way and time to get to know your children and spouse better.

🚗 The Ungame is a game I highly recommend which encourages conversation. It is a simple deck of cards with questions for everyone to answer. This is a unique way to share opinions and feelings, and it will help you get to know and understand yourself and your family.

🚗 Pack a cooler with lots of snacks, drinks, water, etc.

🚗 Have children's tapes, music, books, etc.

🚗 Let children carry a bag with several of their favorite toys. Have them pack this bag themselves.

🚗 Always pack diapers, wipes, bottles, pacifiers, snacks, etc., for small babies

🚗 Always have sick-sacks, towels, wipettes, and changes of clothes. Children often get motion sickness.

🚗 Make sure car seats are safety approved and never let children ride in someone's lap. In most states, it is against the law not to have small children in a car seat.

🚗 Encourage children to nap

When my daughter, Ginnie, drives to visit me, she leaves very early in the morning, before her children are fully awake. After two to three hours, they all stop to wash faces, brush teeth, dress, and have breakfast. This works great, because everyone has traveled several hours and the children were sleeping. I suggest stopping at a rest stop for this break. The children will have a place to run and stretch before continuing their journey.

My daughter, Rebecca, who has three small children, gave me this tip which I think is wonderful!

At meal time, don't stop at a fast food restaurant and let the children eat in the car. This creates a disaster! Take them into the restaurant and leave all the mess behind instead of in your car! This keeps your car from smelling like french fries for the rest of the trip and gives the children stretch and potty time.

Another alternative is to drive through, get your food, and then take it to a rest stop to eat. This lets the children eat and get exercise at the same stop. I do have smart children!

More and more parents are taking their children with them when traveling. Fine hotels and resorts are aware of this growing tendency and many have designed special programs for children.

Check out these hotel programs for children. They will provide more fun time for you and your companion!

- The Radisson—Family Magic Program

- Holiday Inn—Focuses on current happenings for kids

- Howard Johnson's—Kids Ho-Jo Program

- Marriott—Weekend Getaway

- Ritz-Carlton—The Ritz Kids

I recommend staying in suites with children. They are usually roomier with separate living quarters and small kitchenettes.

When on the road, let older children help with navigation and driving.

For older children who want to travel on their own during summer months, did you know that you can stay in dorm rooms in over 300 universities in the United States? The moderate cost is about $20 per night for a clean room and use of campus facilities—a great way to spend some summer time traveling. For information write:

Campus Travel Services
PO Box 8355
Newport Beach, CA 92660

For a fabulous family cruise, see Section VIII - Disney Magic.

You can always go to a
museum, rain or shine.

TRAVELING WITH PETS

In memory of Edisto Hugonot Harvin "Hugo" Boykin Spaniel 1980-1995

TRAVELING WITH PETS

As a pet owner, you have a humane love and responsibility to take precautions to ensure the well-being of your animal while traveling.

If you are traveling via car with your pet, make appropriate stops for water, food, and potty.

When you are traveling on an airline with your pet, be aware of all these tips:

Dog Gone, (407) 569-8434, a newsletter loaded with tips for travelers with pets.

- ❧ Airlines usually require health certificates. Have a veterinarian examine you pet prior to your travels.

- ❧ Have written instructions for your pet's food and water schedule

- ❧ Do not bring dogs or cats to the airline more than 4 hours before departure

- ❧ Dogs and cats must be at least eight weeks old and weaned

- ❧ Animals must be shipped in pressurized locations

- ❧ Pets may be transported as baggage or shipped as cargo

- ❧ Do not feed your pet 4-6 hours prior to a flight. Give a moderate amount of water.

- Try to schedule non-stop flights

- Reserve a space for your pet

- Put your name and your pet's name, address, and phone number on your kennel

- Don't ship pet during extreme hot or cold weather

- Plan your pet's travels carefully. The Humane Society of America has received complaints about almost every airline. Pets are only considered a piece of checked baggage.

- Have your pet travel as carry-on baggage whenever possible. It will have the same rights as you do.

- An animal is checked baggage from a legal liability standpoint

- For serious pet travelers, I suggest <u>Vacationing With Your Pet</u> by Eileen Barish

An internet site for anyone who wants to travel with their dog is TravelDog™. Their internet address is:

http://www.traveldog.com/homepage/homebase.htm

or write

TravelDog™

P.O.Box 19724

Sacramento, CA 95819-0724

Fax 916-455-3476

My most highly recommended suggestion regarding your pet and travel—leave them at home when convenient. Have a pet sitter at your home or board your pet. Pet care facilities now offer country club environments for your pets. Send your pet on a vacation, too!

EATING WHILE TRAVELING

Remember the saying, "You can never be too rich or too thin." If you follow a few simple rules about eating when traveling, you will come home still thin but maybe not too rich!

I could devote many pages on how to eat low-fat, low-sodium, low-calorie, no-sugar, etc., while vacationing, but a vacation is no fun with rigid rules. I want you to have a good time and enjoy eating. You can do this by following a few of my simple and sensible guidelines:

Order foods that are boiled, broiled, roasted, poached, grilled, steamed, or baked.

Try to avoid foods that are fried, creamed, breaded, or scalloped.

Go for marinara sauces.

Order dressing on the side, or fat free dressings.

Order shrimp, crab, oyster cocktails, fruit salads, vegetable salads.

Select steamed vegetables.

Order baked potatoes.

Eat lots of delicious breads without butter.

Eat a healthy breakfast.

Split a dessert with your dinner partner.

Avoid mini-bar food.

Pass up the airline nuts-ask for the pretzels.

Splurge whenever you get the urge! Just don't do this three meals a day!

Many restaurants offer ❤ healthy selections that are delicious. Give them a try.

My favorite way to eat when traveling via car is to pack your own picnic. Picnicking is particularly fun and relaxing when your surroundings are scenic.

See, you have lots of eating choices while traveling.

You don't have to follow any of these suggestions while traveling if you don't want to. Just make sure that you return to a healthy eating lifestyle when you get home.

Try to avoid fast-food restaurants on a regular schedule; however, there are many healthy choices at lots of fast food restaurants.

Here is my fast-food guideline for you. Keep it in your glove compartment.

MY BEST FAST FOOD CHOICES

ARBY'S

Light Roast Chicken Deluxe Sandwich
Light Roast Turkey Deluxe Sandwich
Grilled Chicken Barbecue Sandwich
Baked Potato, plain
Blueberry Muffin
Garden Salad
Roast Chicken Salad
Side Salad
Soup:
    Beef with Vegetable and Barley
    French Onion
    Old Fashion Chicken Noodle
    Tomato Florentine

BURGER KING

Chunky Chicken Salad
Garden Salad
Side Salad
BK Broiler Chicken Sandwich/no mayo

CARL JR'S

Baked Potato-lite
Blueberry Muffin
Bran Muffin
Charbroiler Chicken Salad

Charbroiler BBQ Chicken Sandwich
English Muffin - without butter
Garden Salad

CRACKER BARREL

This is not a fast food restaurant but I also recommend it, because it is a big chain and very accessible.

A choice of entrees, vegetable, salads, fruits and breads.

DAIRY QUEEN/BRAZIER

BBQ Beef Sandwich
DQ Sandwich
Mr. Misty
Side Salad
Strawberry Breeze Yogurt
Yogurt Cone
Yogurt Cup
Yogurt Strawberry Sundae

DUNKIN DONUTS

Muffins - apple 'n spice, banana nut, blueberry, bran with raisin, cranberry, oat bran
Variety of bagels

GOLDEN CORRAL - QUINCEY'S

Although these are not fast food restaurants, I recommend them; because they are numerous, easy to find, and the food is delicious. The atmosphere is relaxing and the rest rooms are shiny clean.

Many low-fat entrees
Vegetable Salad
Fruit Salads
Vegetable
Homemade bread that is delicious

HARDEES
Combo Sub
Grilled Chicken Salad (no dressing)
Ham Sub
Mashed Potatoes
Plain Bagel
Plain Pancakes
Roast Beef Sub
Side Salad
Turkey Sub

LONG JOHN SILVERS
Green Beans
Rice Pilaf
Ocean Chef Salad
Seafood Salad
Side Salad

LOW-FAT LONG JOHN'S MEALS
1-Light Portion Baked Fish with paprika, 2 pieces with rice pilaf and small salad
2-Light portion Baked Fish with lemon crumbs, 2 pieces with rice pilaf and small salad

MCDONALD'S

McDonald's has long been the leader among fast-food restaurants. Most assuredly, you have no excuse for not having accessibility to the golden arches. Approximately 9,000 McDonald's grace America, with another 4,000 in foreign countries. A new McDonald's opens its doors somewhere every 15 hours.

For a low-fat breakfast, you have lots to choose from at McDonald's:

All juices
Carrot Sticks
Celery Sticks
Cheerios
English Muffins (request no butter- use jelly only)
Frozen Yogurt Cup, low-fat vanilla
Frozen Yogurt Sundae, low-fat strawberry
Hot Cakes and Syrup (omit butter)
Milk Shake, low-fat strawberry-chocolate
Muffin, fat-free apple bran muffin, fat-free blueberry
Muffin, fat-free blueberry bran muffin
Garden Salad
Side Salad
Wheaties
Orange Sorbet Ice, cup or sundae
Low-Fat Frozen Yogurt Twist Cup or Sundae

SUBWAY

Subway sandwich shops are multiplying faster than just about any other fast-food chain in the country.

Subway will make a sandwich from 3-100 feet long at the cost of about $12 per foot. Have you ever had a $1200 sandwich? Why don't you try it for your next party? Make sure that you have a long table!

Large Garden Salad
Small Turkey Salad
Turkey Sandwich (6 inch)
Ham Sandwich
Roast Beef Sandwich (6 inch)
Club Sandwich (6 inch)

WENDYS

I believe that Wendy's salad bar is the best in the fast-food business.

Load up on all vegetable and fruits with a low-fat dressing. Spaghetti and/or Spanish rice along with your salad makes a delicious low-fat fast food meal.

All fruits
All vegetables
Baked Potato, plain
Pasta Salad
Refried Beans
Spaghetti Sauce
Spanish Rice
Turkey Ham (from salad bar)

ICE CREAM SHOPS
BASKIN ROBBINS
Fat-Free Chocolate Vanilla Twist
Non-Fat Frozen Yogurt
Fat-Free Just Peach (frozen dairy dessert)
Rainbow Sherbet
Fruit Whip Sorbet
Red Raspberry Sorbet
Sugar-Free Dairy Dessert, Chunky Banana

TCBY
Non-fat frozen yogurts
Sugar-free frozen yogurts

There are many more fast-food chains. I listed the most popular in my area. Choose one wisely.

Remember, the same rules that you use at other restaurants apply at fast food restaurants.

Ask for low-fat or no-fat dressing for your garden salad, or, better yet, bring your own no-fat dressing. Otherwise, you will ruin a good thing with several hundred additional fat calories.

Avoid fatty condiments and sauces at that baked potato bar. As with the salad, you can make a very healthy food unhealthy. Choose no-fat toppings from the salad bar, or again, bring you own dressing. Keep in mind that lemon juice is delicious on a baked potato.

Omit the mayonnaise, tartar sauce, and cheese on those chicken and fish sandwiches and hamburgers. Substitute lemon juice, ketchup, and mustard.

Above all, never, never order anything fried at a fast-food restaurant. Some restaurants will promote these high-profit items by inquiring after your order is given if you want fries and/or onion rings. Always say no and you will save yourself a lot of fat calories.

If you are interested in a complete basic guide to a fat-free and low fat lifestyle of eating, I recommend my first book, <u>Don't Butter Me Up!</u> This book tells you in simple language how to get started, what to buy, how to cook, etc. <u>Don't Butter Me Up!</u> has 2 complete-21 day meal plans with all recipes included.

<u>Don't Butter Me Up!</u> may be ordered by any bookstore (distributor Ingram),

or from:
Rebecca Enterprises
986 Meadow Lane
Henderson NC 27536
919-438-8849
$14.95 + $2.00 postage.

Now you have your guidelines for eating healthy while traveling. Remember, I said I want you to have a good time and enjoy eating. Splurge when you get the urge—occasionally!

EAT   EAT   EAT

CRUISES
AND
SPECIAL INTEREST

CRUISES

Planning a cruise is not as easy as many people imagine. Just the contrary—a cruise should be extremely well planned. Once you are on board, it is impossible to change your plans. Without thorough plans, you could be stuck with an unpleasant vacation from 5-10 days.

Before you cruise—choose:

- A good travel agent experienced in cruise travel

- A cruise line ship and itinerary that suits you

- The location of your stateroom

A good travel agent will be knowledgeable about cruise lines and their ports of call.

Cruise lines and ship selections have distinct personalities. Do you want a party till dawn atmosphere, or an early, do the swing with Benny Goodman night?

Cruise ships have different itinerary selections. Many cruise ships sail the same routes with the same ports of call. If you want to visit unusual out-of-the ordinary ports, you will have to select the right cruise line. Select a cruise ship that will have ports of call that suit you.

Remember, port stops are brief, but these short visits will help you decide if you would like to pursue a longer visit.

After you have selected your travel agent, your ship and your itinerary, study your ships deck plan. There are many staterooms to choose from. Choose one that suits you and your budget. Remember that moving up in price does not necessarily get you a bigger room, only a better location.

To help you with all these cruise planning decisions I recommend:

<u>Fodor's Cruises and Ports of Call, 1996</u>

or

<u>Fielding's Guide to World Wide Cruises</u>.

These guide books are excellent and will give you detailed information on cruising.

NEWEST CRUISE NEWS
CARNIVAL DESTINY

The world's largest cruise ship, the Carnival Destiny, will set sail in November, 1996.

This new ship, which is too wide to pass through the Panama Canal, will sail year-round in the Caribbean from its base in Miami, Florida.

The ship's architect, Joe Farcus, has created a spectacular "monumentality" to the floating palaces of old. The main lounge, the Palladium, is in the grand ole style with a gold dome and huge chandelier in the center. The Carnival Destiny has many awesome architectural features.

For information:

Carnival Cruise Line 800-327-9501

DISNEY MAGIC

Disney Magic of Disney Cruise Line will launch its first cruise in January of 1998. This cruise sounds fabulous and will offer specialized activities and events for these groups of people: adults, families with children, and seniors.

This cruise will be packaged with three-or four-day stays at Disney World®. Passengers will dine in three different dining rooms, and there will be a restaurant for adults only. This ship will offer: specific programs for 3-12 year olds, a teen club, children's counselors, nightly entertainment, adult enrichment programs, family lounges with family-oriented activities, huge shopping areas, and Disney character "tuck-ins" for children at bedtime!

Sounds like the perfect cruise for the young and the young at heart! You can make your reservation now.

DOFFING YOUR DUDS!

Last but not least, if you have given serious thought to your next vacation but just can't make up your mind, you may want to try this cruise excursion.

You would certainly be able to pack lightly and sleep naked!

I personally have not been on this cruise (I promise Bessie). According to this article, I would be regarded as a "textile."

NUDE CRUISES TAKE OFF
IN POPULARITY

Arline Bleecker
Orlando Sentinel

Most vacationers planning a cruise worry about what to pack. For nudists, such a dilemma is immaterial, and they probably wouldn't worry much if their luggage got lost altogether.

With or without bulging suitcases, nudists are taking to the seas. According to the American Association for Nude Recreation based in Kissimmee, Fla., nude vacationing is one of the fastest growing segments of the North American travel industry. Cruise lines have begun to take notice of the association's 46,000 members. Even ships of Cunard have loosened stuffy dress codes for nude charters.

Nude cruising isn't merely streakers going to sea, though. The focus is on upscale "clothing options" travel. A small percentage of nudists do live and breathe the nudist lifestyle, but for most the attraction is sunbathing, snorkeling and not having to hassle with sand in your bathing suit!

A nude cruise is just like any other cruise, except that once the ship enters international waters, cruisers are free to doff their duds. There is no pressure to take it all off on these cruises, and no tantalization.

Of course, where to stash your lipstick or a stateroom key might pose bigger problems than voyeurism, and shipboard nudity gives new meaning to those "no shorts allowed" signs routinely posted outside main dining rooms. But if full nudity in the dining room sounds like it takes this decree too literally, relax. Preferences for nudity in ships' formal restaurants vary from ship to ship, and the nude vs. food

> ## NUDE CRUISING ADVANTAGES
> Pack Quickly.
> No sand in your bathing suit!

controversy settles out in its own way on each cruise.

In the jargon of nudists, fully clothed folks are referred to as "textiles." Cruises at Halloween are a particular draw, with un-costume parties that are more like Brazil's Carnival—with painted bodies, mask only or topless.

Not surprisingly, warm-weather destinations make for prime itineraries for nude cruises, allowing opportunities to enjoy nude recreation on shore. Excursions include visits to rain forests and waterfalls and river-rafting trips in such lush destinations as Jamaica, Grand-Cayman and the Dominican Republic.

For information concerning these cruises:
Bare Necessities 1-800-743-0405
Travel Au Naturel 1-800-728-0185

You have now learned from my book that most successful travels require lots of planning, more so than lots of money and time…or night clothes!

From
<u>Pack Lightly</u>
<u>Sleep Naked</u>
and
Rebecca Harvin

BON VOYAGE!

SITTERS CHECKLIST

Numbers - addresses where we can be reached

_____

_____

_____

_____

_____

Numbers to call in emergency

Relative	Name	Number
_____	_____	_____
Friend		
_____	_____	_____
Police		
_____		

Fire Department

_____

Child's Doctor

_____

Poison Control Center

_____

Paramedic/Ambulance

_____

Taxi Service

_____

Office

_____

Medication for Child

_____

Food Allergies

_____

WHERE TO FIND

Medicine Cabinet

_____

Fire Exit

_____

Fire Alarms

_____

Fire Extinguishers

_____

PACK LIGHTLY. SLEEP NAKED.

REMINDERS:

Off limits for children

_____

_____

_____

Children's duties are

_____

_____

_____

Sitter's duties are

_____

_____

_____

_____

MY PERSONAL CHECKLIST:

All medicines

_____

Glasses

_____

Contacts

_____

All toiletries

_____

Film

_____

Camera

_____

Sunscreen

_____

Your Personal Favorite Travel Tips

Other Books by Rebecca Harvin

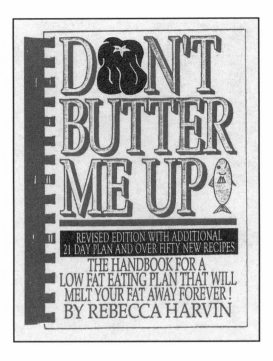

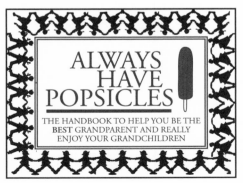

ORDER BLANK
PACK LIGHTLY. SLEEP NAKED.

Rebecca Harvin, 986 Meadow Lane, Henderson, NC 27536
(919) 438-8849

Please send me _____ **copies of** <u>Pack Lightly. Sleep Naked</u>.

_____@ $11.95 per copy, plus $2.00 per book for postage and handling
(call for postage and handling charges for more than three copies.)

My check payable to Rebecca Harvin in the amount of $ _____ is enclosed.

Name _____

Street _____

City _____ State _____ Zip _____

ORDER BLANK
PACK LIGHTLY. SLEEP NAKED.

Rebecca Harvin, 986 Meadow Lane, Henderson, NC 27536
(919) 438-8849

Please send me _____ **copies of** <u>Pack Lightly. Sleep Naked</u>.

_____@ $11.95 per copy, plus $2.00 per book for postage and handling
(call for postage and handling charges for more than three copies.)

My check payable to Rebecca Harvin in the amount of $ _____ is enclosed.

Name _____

Street _____

City _____ State _____ Zip _____